D1716335

WITCHES

CYNTHIA A. ROBY

Cavendish
Square

New York

CREATURES OF FANTASY

Witches

BY

CYNTHIA A. ROBY

CAVENDISH SQUARE PUBLISHING · NEW YORK

Published in 2016 by Cavendish Square Publishing, LLC
243 5th Avenue, Suite 136, New York, NY 10016

Library of Congress Cataloging-in-Publication Data

Roby, Cynthia.
Witches / Cynthia A. Roby.
pages cm. — (Creatures of fantasy)
Includes bibliographical references and index.
ISBN 978-1-5026-0930-4 (hardcover) ISBN 978-1-5026-0931-1 (ebook)
1. Witches—Juvenile literature. 2. Witchcraft—Juvenile literature. I. Title.
BF1566.R557 2016
133.4'3—dc23
2015029123

Editorial Director: David McNamara
Editor: Kristen Susienka
Copy Editor: Nathan Heidelberger
Art Director: Jeffrey Talbot
Designer: Joseph Macri
Senior Production Manager: Jennifer Ryder-Talbot
Production Editor: Renni Johnson
Photo Research: J8 Media

Printed in the United States of America

CONTENTS

For centuries, witches and witchcraft have captivated curious minds. They have been seen as objects of wisdom and evil in folklore for many generations.

INTRODUCTION

Since the first humans walked the earth, myths and legends have engaged minds and inspired imaginations. Ancient civilizations used stories to explain phenomena in the world around them: the weather, tides, and natural disasters. As different cultures evolved, so too did their stories. From their traditions and observations emerged creatures with powerful abilities, mythical intrigue, and their own origins. Sometimes, different cultures encouraged various manifestations of the same creature. At other times, these creatures and cultures morphed into entirely new beings with greater powers than their predecessors.

Today, societies still celebrate the folklore of their ancestors—on-screen in presentations such as *The Hobbit, The Walking Dead,* and *X-Men*; and in stories such as *Harry Potter* and *Twilight*. Some even believe these creatures truly existed and continue to walk the earth as living creatures. Others resign these beings to myth.

In the Creatures of Fantasy series, we celebrate captivating stories of the past from all around the world. Each book focuses on creatures both familiar and unknown: the terrifying ghost, the bloodthirsty vampire, the classic Frankenstein, mischievous goblins, enchanting witches, and the callous zombie. Here their various incarnations throughout history are brought to life. All have their own origins, their own legends, and their own influences on the imagination today. Each story adds a new perspective to the human experience and encourages people to revisit tales of the past in order to understand their presence in the modern age.

HISTORY AND HYSTERIA

"Perhaps I am the only person who, asked whether she were a witch or not, could truthfully say, I do not know. I do know some very strange things have happened to me, or through me."

LADY ALICE ROWHEDGE, FROM NORAH LOFTS'S *BLESS THIS HOUSE*

NCE UPON A TIME, THERE WAS A woman who lived on the outskirts of her village near the forest. She was young, independent, and alone. Her small cottage was nestled within a garden filled with animals she befriended, herbs, and other healing plants. Taught by nature, she held a keen **mystical** knowledge concerning life. A midwife, she helped women give birth. With healing hands, she prepared herbs that cured the sick. Her medical knowledge threatened the village doctor. Her simple spiritual values threatened members of the village's church. Her independence and freedom stirred up jealousy among women and caused men to hate her—thus her life was doomed to be disrupted.

Opposite: This engraving shows the burning of a sixteenth-century Dutch woman as a heretic or witch. The majority of those suspected of witchcraft were women.

In the middle of the night, the **Inquisition**, with torches and axes and ropes in hand, descended upon the small cottage. The young woman was cruelly tortured into confessing lies about the devil. After, she was burned alive. Her crime: according to the villagers, she was a witch. Was she good? Was she evil? Did she cast spells to cause bad things to happen? The truth is that the answers never mattered. Witches and witchcraft were feared.

Defining the "Witch"

This story holds true for thousands of sixteenth-century so-called witches. It is a tale that has been told and retold, in full or in part, by academics, poets, novelists, historians, theologians, and dramatists. These stories are compelling and even horrifying, yet they are mostly true accounts of what happened to the women, and many men, dubbed witches in the early modern period.

The nature and history of witches is complicated. Centuries ago, it was widely believed that a witch had sold her soul to the devil in exchange for evil powers, such as the ability to harm others. Although this stereotype may have been true of some sects, many modern-day witches argue that it does not represent their beliefs.

The term "witch" is based on traditional magic and ghost beliefs. Its first known use was before the twelfth century CE. The word derives from the Old English words "wicca" and "wicce" (masculine and feminine forms, respectively). The origin of these words is not entirely known, but scholars have suggested that they initially meant "wise one."

Wicca and wicce later became "wicche" in Middle English and held the same meaning. At that time, however, wicche could be used to refer to either a man or a woman. As time went on, words

such as wizard, sorcerer, and warlock arose to distinguish a male witch from a female one. Wicche later changed to "witch" by the sixteenth century. At this point, a witch was exclusively female. In the **Wiccan** religion, it is common to refer to both men and women as witches. In this case, though, "witch" simply refers to an **adherent** of Wicca.

Do Witches Exist?

The most common misconception about witchcraft is there is no such thing as a witch. Some consider the subject silly and trivial. Those who do not believe in the existence of witches may describe them as imaginary old hags with warts on their noses, cone-shaped hats, broomsticks, black cats, and evil, cackling laughs. They even imagine that witches practice forms of **voodoo** through supernatural powers. Others argue that witches are alive, possess psychic abilities, and are active in today's society. In fact, Wicca is considered a recognized religion by a number of institutions, including the United States military and the US legal system. The anthropological approach is that a witch is a sorcerer. According to the historical approach to European witchcraft, a witch worships the devil. However, favored by most modern witches is that a witch worships gods and goddesses and practices magic for good ends.

Black Magic, White Magic, and Fear

Belief in magic and witchcraft has existed since humans first walked on the earth. Early man worshipped the gods and goddesses he believed controlled his world. During good times, these deities gifted humans with large harvests and mild winters. During bad

These three women, accused of practicing witchcraft, were executed in Derneburg, Germany, in October 1555.

times, in which bad weather, famines, and plagues tormented people, man turned to magic. People sought relief from sorcerers, shamans, witches, and other individuals gifted with magic who could harness, or put to work, the power of the gods. This power to either protect or destroy gave witches, who were mostly women, a complicated reputation. On the one hand, they were seen as wise healers. On the other, people feared the power they wielded.

Fear of so-called witches and witchcraft was rampant throughout Europe during the **Middle Ages**. During this time, there was thought to be two different types of magic. One was white magic, which was associated with faith in God and was thought to stem from religious symbols and nature. White magic was used for beneficial purposes: love spells, healing potions, talismans for wealth, and more.

The other type of magic was much more sinister: black magic. The source of black magic was the devil. People feared witches because they were imagined to wield black magic. Witches threatened society through their use of black magic, cursing individuals and causing bad things to happen to them. If someone fell ill from unknown causes or suffered an accident, people often blamed witches.

The distinction between white and black magic was so much a part of society that it was even incorporated into Roman law. If someone was convicted of using black magic for any crime less than murder, for example, the punishment might include a fine, jail time, or banishment. Roman law sanctioned the use of white magic, though, for such purposes as healing and **divination**.

Malleus Maleficarum

In 1486, two German monks, James Sprenger and Heinrich Kramer, published *Malleus Maleficarum*, or *Hammer of Witches*. The **treatise** listed the supernatural acts performed by witches and told how witches caused disease, destroyed crops, and kidnapped and ate innocent children. The monks also explain why witches are more apt to be female than male:

First [women] are more **credulous** ... therefore [the devil] attacks them ... Second ... women are naturally more impressionable, and more ready to receive the influence of a disembodied spirit, and that when they use this quality well they are very good, but when they use it badly they are very evil ... Third [women] have slippery tongues, and are unable to conceal from their fellow-women those things which they know through their evil arts. And since they are weak, they find a secret and easy manner of vindicating themselves by witchcraft ... Since they are feebler both in mind and body, it is not surprising that they should come more under the spell of witchcraft. For as regards intellect, of the understanding of spiritual things, they seem to be of a different nature than men ... It should be noted that there was a defect in the formation of the first woman, since she was formed from a bent rib ... since through this defect she is an imperfect animal, she always deceives.

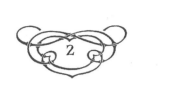

BEFORE SALEM

"The blackest chapter in the history of witchcraft lies not in the malevolence of witches but in the deliberate, gloating cruelty of their prosecutors."

THEDA KENYON, *WITCHES STILL LIVE*

THE HISTORY OF WITCHES AND WITCHCRAFT can be either endlessly fascinating or intellectually frustrating. The subject itself conjures diverse images. On one hand, it summons thoughts of old age, frightful ugliness, and female wickedness. On the other are youth, beauty, and feminine skills in outwitting. It all began before Salem, the place where the most dramatic episodes involving witches and witchcraft would eventually take place.

EARLY WITCHES

Witches and witchcraft have been a part of human cultures for millennia, dating back to man's earliest time. Simple **sorcery**, such

Opposite: The practices of witchcraft and invocation have been around since ancient times.

as using charms or making offerings to spirits, is a common feature across most traditional societies. Many prehistoric cave paintings, for example, depict magic rituals. These are often closely associated with other cave paintings depicting animal hunts, suggesting that magic rituals were performed to either guarantee or celebrate a successful hunt. Perhaps the oldest religion in the world is shamanism, the practice of communicating with spirits through dreams and meditation.

Witches were common in the ancient civilizations of Sumeria and Babylonia. These cultures believed that the world was full of hostile spirits. Although every person had their own spirit that could help protect them from such evil spirits, it was up to witches to combat these demons directly through their use of magic.

Other ancient peoples, such as the Egyptians, the Hebrews, the Greeks, and the Romans, influenced later Western beliefs about witchcraft. Egyptian witches, for example, bent the cosmos to their wills through amulets, spells, formulas, and even math. The knowledge recorded by Egyptian witches helped to inform later European alchemists seeking to adjust the chemical composition of elements and create healing potions. The Egyptians also used magical **incantations**, which were inscribed on various amulets and other items. Many examples of these magic items have been recovered by archaeologists.

Ancient Greeks went one step further in the use of magic, incorporating it into many aspects of their religion. One type of magic, known as *theurgy*, included magical rituals, which were performed in the hopes of invoking the power of the gods. Other times, these rituals were performed to unite one's soul with the gods, thereby achieving divine perfection. The Greeks also had

another form of magic called *mageia*. Similar to sorcery, mageia was a more practical type of magic. Those who used mageia were thought to have powers to directly help or harm others. This type of magic is most similar to the powers that witches in Europe during the Middle Ages were feared to possess.

Convicted of Dark Magic

For years Ireland held more of a relaxed attitude about witchcraft than mainland Europe. However, witch hunts eventually arrived there, too. One of the first and most notorious hunt victims was Dame Alice Kyteler (circa 1280–ca. 1325), a wealthy moneylender whose husbands had a mysterious habit of dying and leaving everything to her. In fact, it was around the time that her fourth husband, John Le Poer, was preparing his will—a document that promised his riches to Kyteler—that his fingernails, for no reason, began to fall off. The people of Kilkenny, Ireland, became suspicious. An account of Le Poer in 1324 noted that he was deathly thin and his hair had fallen out, symptoms of arsenic poisoning.

Not all the facts of Kyteler's case are clear, but what is known is that Le Poer had three children—all of whom Kyteler disinherited. As Le Poer continued to waste away, he and the children began to suspect Kyteler of foul play. In fact, the truth about whether Kyteler was involved in the deaths of all of her husbands remains cause for speculation. Regardless, the people of Kilkenny talked, and at the time, suspicion was enough to accuse Kyteler of and try her for witchcraft.

In 1324, church officials put Kyteler on trial. The charge was heading a secret society of **heretical** sorcerers. She was not only the first person on Irish soil to be accused of witchcraft but also the

An engraving of St. Canice's Cathedral in Kilkenny, Ireland

first who had been directly accused of having a relationship with an **incubus**. Kilkenny authorities, on many occasions, attempted to imprison Kyteler, but she was rich and well connected—always managing to escape. According to the stories told, Le Poer and his children went to a home that Kyteler owned on the seaside. There they found "terrible items," all suggesting that Kyteler was in fact practicing "the dark arts." There were gruesome pieces of evidence that included evil powders, the fingernails and toenails of corpses boiled in the skull of a robber, and candles made of human fat. The Le Poer family packed the items into crates and brought them to the bishop of Ossory, Richard de Ledrede. However, the Lord Chancellor of Ireland was Kyteler's brother-in-law. When Bishop de Ledrede visited Kyteler to investigate the charges, she used her influence with the Lord Chancellor to imprison the bishop for seventeen days. Once released, he was certain to see that Kyteler was prosecuted. Kyteler's fate was in his hands. Kyteler, her son William, and ten others were convicted.

Kyteler's maidservant, Petronilla de Meath (ca. 1300–1324), was put to death by burning. After being flogged and tortured, she confessed to practicing witchcraft and implicated Kyteler. William was sentenced to attend mass three times per day for a year as well as perform charitable tasks, including feeding the poor and repairing the roof of Saint Canice's Cathedral. It was said that he did the job poorly. The other nine were burned to death.

Kyteler's Charges

Seven charges, ranging from committing sorcery and demonism to having murdered several husbands, were brought against Kyteler. She was also accused of having illegally acquired her wealth through witchcraft. Bishop Richard de Ledrede read the charges against her at the trial:

> That they were denying Christ and the church; that they cut up living animals and scattered the pieces at crossroads as offerings to a [demon]; that they stole the keys of the church and held meetings there at night; that in the skull of a robber they placed the intestines and internal organs of cocks, worms, nails cut from dead bodies; that, from this brew they made potions to incite people to love, hate, kill and afflict Christians; that [Kyteler] herself had a certain demon as incubus; and that [Kyteler] had used her sorcery to murder some of her husbands and to infatuate others, with the result that they gave all of their possessions to her and her son.

On the night before the burning, Kyteler disappeared. According to some accounts, she went to England where she lived in luxury until her natural death. Whether she actually dabbled in the dark arts or not, she is remembered to this day as Ireland's first witch.

Bewitching to Death

Agnes Waterhouse (1503–1566), also known as Mother Waterhouse, was England's first woman executed for practicing witchcraft. In 1566, she was accused of bewitching to death

William Fynne and using sorcery to kill livestock, cause illness, and cause the death of her husband. Two other women at that time, Elizabeth Francis and Joan Waterhouse, were also charged. The trio of so-called witches were from the same English village: Hatfield Peverel. The strange thing about the case was that the church had nothing to do with accusing Mother Waterhouse—she was the first English witch sentenced to death by a **secular** court.

In giving her testimony, Mother Waterhouse admitted to practicing the dark arts and to devil worship. Many of the sixty-four-year-old's horrifying admissions at the Examination and Confession of Certain Witches at Chelmsford in the County of Essex, before the Queen Majesty's Judges, were recorded by Frank Luttmer:

> First she received this cat of this Francis's wife in the order as is before said, who willed her to call him Satan, and told her that if she made much of him he would do for her what she would have him to do … When she had received him she (to try him what he could do) willed him to kill a hog of her own which he did, and she gave him for his labor a chicken, which he first required of her and a drop of her blood … She took her cat Satan in her lap and put him in the wood before her door, and willed him to kill three of this Father Kersey's hogs … [After] falling out with one Widow Gooday she willed Satan to drown her cow and he did so, and she rewarded him as before … [On] falling out with another of her neighbors, she killed her three geese in the same manner.

Mother Waterhouse was unrepentant, stating that Satan had told her she would die by hanging or burning and there was not a lot she could do about it. She was hanged at Chelmsford in England on July 29, 1566.

The Bell Witch Haunting

The Bell Witch was a **poltergeist** that lived in the Robertson County, Tennessee, home of John Bell Sr. in 1817. The witch would attack members of the Bell family and frequently swear at them.

During the night, the Bells began hearing faint, whispering voices. Soon, the witch turned its attention on Betsy, the Bells' youngest daughter. The witch started to physically attack Betsy, pulling her hair and slapping her, which left marks on her face and body. John Bell turned to his neighbor James Johnston for help.

To witness the Bell house events, Johnston and his wife spent the night there. Throughout the night, they experienced strange activity. At one point, Johnston's bedcovers were stripped away and Johnston himself slapped. Johnston jumped out of bed and demanded to know who was attacking him. He got no reply back, but the activity stopped for the night.

The home of John Bell Sr. and his family in Robertson County, Tennessee

The Bell Witch did not cease terrorizing the house, however. On December 20, 1820, John Bell mysteriously died. Shortly after, the Bells found a vial of strange liquid in the cupboard. In the hopes of figuring out what it was, John Bell Jr. gave a drop of it to the family's cat, which died instantly. The family then heard a disembodied voice say, "I gave Ol' Jack a big dose of that last night, which fixed him!" John Jr. threw the remainder of poison into the fireplace, which burst into a strange, blue flame that escaped through the chimney.

HOCUS POCUS: THE MAGIC OF WITCHES

"There are some secrets darker than witchcraft."

APRIL AASHEIM, *THE WITCHES OF DARK ROOT*

T HE WORD "MAGIC" COMES FROM THE Persian and Greek roots *magus* and *magos*, which mean "wise." These words are also tied to the English word "magi," which means "wise men." Magic has been a part of every culture's experience. Magic-makers throughout the centuries and in every culture have played similar roles and held similar characteristics. Whether they were called witches, shamans, sages, or mystics, they were skilled at healing the sick, growing crops, assisting at births, and tracking the influence of stars and planets. They have used their powers for a variety of goals, good and bad, for themselves and for others.

Opposite: A woman casts a love potion while her cat sits at her feet.

23

Danger or Illusion?

Witches have historically made headlines, often in conflict with Christian churches, but not all witches have ill intentions. One may pass them on the street without knowing it. They don't wear pointed hats and ride brooms but look like the rest of society. They are trained in the art and work, live, and play among non-witches. However, Doreen Valiente, a practicing witch in Great Britain, believes that witchcraft should never be approached lightly. She says, "The event of silly dabbling in the occult that goes on today scares me. These people think they're doing something terribly clever and terribly witty and it's all great fun. But what they don't understand is that they are invoking forces ... They are making themselves a channel through which those forces can come through into the world."

The Color of Magic

Movies, television programs, and video games have often used colors to indicate different types of magic. A love potion may appear pink or red, while a spell may manifest as green to denote the caster's greed. And of course, the medieval distinction between white (good) and black (evil) magic still frequently applies.

Black magic, dark magic, dark side magic—these are all forms of magic or sorcery that draw on **malevolent** powers. These types of evil magic may be used to bring misfortune or harm to others—such as unexplained illnesses or freak accidents. In more popular usages, the term "black magic" may describe any form of ritual that one group or person disapproves of or finds unnatural and foreign. Outside of popular literature, black magic usually refers to magic utilized for gaining power and wealth or taking revenge for evil's sake.

Middle Eastern religions typically disapproved of black magic regardless of if the established religion was monotheistic or polytheistic (a belief in a single god or in many gods, respectively) because it made its victims unable to contribute to society. White, or protective, magic generally refers to healing and its use has never been discouraged. Distinctions between the two are debatable.

Most branches of the major religions of Christianity, Islam, Judaism, and Hinduism would likely argue that all forms of magic, regardless of their origins, are evil. Others may argue that all magic is essentially the same; white magic may have a bad outcome, and black magic may have a good one. Another view is that any spell, based on its end result, could be either black or white.

Gray magic is a little-used term describing magic that is performed neither for beneficial nor malevolent reasons. Gray magic borders in the continuum between black and white magic. Its practitioners, dubbed gray witches, view magic as a neutral means to either positive or negative ends.

WEIRD SISTERS

Witches have not been confined only to the realm of myths and religion. They have also found their way into literature. Many of the world's greatest writers have found inspiration in witches, including the English poet and playwright William Shakespeare. Shakespeare's *Macbeth* features not one but three witches, who use their bizarre powers to influence the events of the play. Shakespeare penned *Macbeth* just nine years after King James passed an anti-witchcraft law, which remained in effect for more than 130 years.

The *Macbeth* witches, dubbed the Weird Sisters, possess many supernatural powers, including fortune telling and apparition

creation, which help set the tragic events of the play in motion. Throughout the play, the witches drudge up centuries of mischief with—unbeknownst to anyone at that time—the black magic incantations spoken onstage.

Double, Double, Toil and Trouble

Its spooky characters are not the only superstitious aspect of *Macbeth*. Today, it is common for actors to refer to *Macbeth* as "The Scottish Play" because theater lore holds that the play is cursed. Many performances of the play throughout history have been fraught with disaster, from actors suffering injuries onstage to riots and deaths surrounding the production. It's no wonder why the curse of The Scottish Play is one of the most enduring superstitions of the stage, and many actors take it seriously.

There are several alleged explanations for the curse. One holds that Shakespeare used real witches' incantations for the Weird Sisters' lines, infusing his play with dark magic.

Another legend says that Shakespeare wrote *Macbeth* in honor of his king and patron, James VI of Scotland, who had authored the 1599 book *Daemonologie*, which supports the practice of witch hunting. Shakespeare incorporated excerpts from James's book, hoping to please his patron. The legend maintains that some practicing witches who attended the play were offended by its anti-witchcraft language. Hoping to dissuade anyone from performing the play again, these witches placed a curse on the play and whomever might perform it. Whenever *Macbeth* is performed and an actor says the name of the play, it is said that the witches—either the Weird Sisters themselves or those who had attended Shakespeare's performance—are awoken, descending on the playhouse to wreak havoc.

This painting
shows Macbeth
and Banquo
meeting the
three witches
on a heath in
Macbeth.

Alakazam!

Transformation spells are said to change objects, people, or animals into something different—but careful, a reverse spell is important. The effects are said to be permanent without it. Here are a few common spells, according to the *Book of Shadows* by N. E. Genge:

To shrink something: *Shrinkus Minisculus*!

To make something really tall: *Maximus*!

To make something really small: *Minimus*!

To make someone say what they really think: *Compello Placalo, Veritas Adultrum*!

To teleport people or yourself around: *Hocus Pocus, Habeas Corpus*!

Above: This engraving shows a wizard performing spells in his den.

To turn a person into a pig: *Alverix Orcus, Transfrogamorphus, Spotticus, Trotticus, Transferus Porcus!*

To turn a person into a donkey: *Alverix Orcus, Transfrogamorphus, Floppylog Donkeybrae, Transferus Asinae!*

To turn a person into a dog: *Alverix Orcus, Transdogamorphus, Woofus Rufus, Transfurrus Muttus!*

To turn a person into a chicken: *Alverix Orcus, Transfrogamorphus, Illio Allio, Poultus Transformus!*

To turn people into frogs or toads: *Alverix Orcus, Transfrogamorphus, Rufus Rofus, Randaiprophus!*

To turn a person into a turkey: *Alverix Orcus, Transfrogamorphus, Wickety Wackety, Gabblus Gorkus!*

To turn anything into food: *Alacazam, Alacazoo!*

To change something into a balloon: *Expando Extendarae, Baloonus Disdendari!*

To change a balloon into a bunch of flowers: *Intrenso Profundus, Baloonus Floribundus!*

To change toadstools into flowers: *Crysanthamun Maximum, Rubbelum Grandiflorum!*

To change someone's hairstyle: *Crimpus Cuttus, Primpus Permus, Mousseus Chopus, Punkus Topus!*

To transform an inanimate object into a bird: *Objectus Inertus, Areatus Convertus!*

To turn a person into a statue: (name here), *Transmutatae, Corpus Vitae, Terracotta!*

FROM PARANOIA TO PARDON

*"Would it do any good to open Aunt Sarai's grave and drive
a stake through her? If you believe in as much sorcery as
that, you must regret the days of witch-burners."*

EVANGELINE WALTON, *WITCH HOUSE*

THE SPRING OF 1692 BROUGHT CHAOS to the small village of Salem, Massachusetts. A group of young girls who had been behaving strangely complained that they were being tormented by the devil. Each of them accused several local women of being witches. The accusations set Salem and several surrounding towns ablaze with hysteria. Paranoid citizens accused a total of 162 people. Fifty-two people were tried, thirty were condemned, and twenty were put to death. Nineteen of the deaths were by hanging and one man was crushed to death by heavy stones. At least five more died in prison. As bad as the Salem witch trials were, however, it was only one of many such witch hunts.

Opposite: This illustration depicts events during a Salem witch trial.

MALICIOUS MALADIES

Between 1689 and 1690, residents of a northeastern Massachusetts colony began to report experiencing malicious **maladies**. They complained of convulsions, hallucinations, psychosis, pin-prickling bites on their skin, lethargy, and mysterious deaths. Some said they "barked like dogs." Others reported being unable to walk; their arms and legs "nearly twisted out of joint." In late winter and early spring of 1692, residents of Salem Village, Massachusetts, suffered the same random and unexplained illnesses. The livestock, too, began to suffer. With the limited scientific and medical knowledge of the time, physicians who were consulted offered one diagnosis: witchcraft. Such a diagnosis drove the residents of northeastern Massachusetts to experience a succession of witchcraft accusations that resulted in witch hunts, hearings, trials, imprisonments, and executions.

THE WITCH CRAZE

The age of witch hunting swept from Germany to England from the fourteenth to the seventeenth centuries. Though it took on different forms at different times and places, one fact remains constant: witch hunts were usually led by the aristocracy and targeted female peasants. These alleged witches, people argued, were a threat to not only governments but also the Protestant and Catholic churches.

Thousands of executions took place at this time—most common were burnings at the stake. By the mid-sixteenth century, the terror had jumped from continental Europe to England. Researchers estimate that the executions averaged six hundred per year for certain German cities. During a single year in Wertzberg,

nine hundred so-called witches were killed; in and around Como, one thousand were killed; and in 1585, the Bishopric of Trier had two villages with only one remaining woman each. Women, old and young, made up about 85 percent of those executed.

It is unfortunate that the witches themselves—mostly poor and illiterate—did not document their stories. Like all history, they were recorded by the so-called educated elite. Thus, witches are only known through the eyes of their persecutors.

The Witch Craze Explained

There are two common explanations for the witch craze. One theory states that the **peasantry** was caught up with paranoia. The craze was "an epidemic of mass hatred in panic cast in images of a blood-lusty peasant mob bearing flaming torches." The second version takes a psychological angle, reasoning that the accused witches themselves may have been insane. According to psychiatric historian Gregory Zilboorg, "Millions of witches, sorcerers, possessed and obsessed were an enormous mass of severe neurotics [and] psychotics ... For many years the world looked like [a] veritable insane asylum." Yet the witch craze, in reality, was not the unfortunate result of hysterical women. It followed legal procedures, an organized campaign carried out by church and state.

Rules of the Trial

To Catholics and Protestants, Reverends Kramer and Sprenger's *Hammer of Witches* served as the witch hunter's authoritative guide. This book proved invaluable to judges presiding over witch trials for three centuries. The exhaustive text covered all manner of topics regarding witches and their trials. For example, it was instructed

that a witch trial may only be initiated by a vicar, priest, or judge of the county. Either was tasked to post a notice to local people, asking them to reveal witches or signs of witchcraft within twelve days. Anyone who did not report a suspected witch may be sentenced to any number of **temporal** punishments or worse, **excommunicated**.

If one witch was exposed, testimonies and confessions during her trial could reveal other witches. Kramer and Sprenger therefore provided detailed instruction about the use of torture to force such confessions. A witch's torture often began when she was stripped and her hair shaved. From there, she might be placed in any one of a number of cruel torture devices, such as thumbscrews or the rack, a table where a victim's arms would be tied to ropes, which would be tightened, stretching the body and causing severe pain and injuries.

Illegal Witchery

Who were the witches? What were their crimes? During the centuries of witch hunting, accusations of witchcraft arose for crimes ranging from public indecency to political and religious subversion. However, three activities in particular often led to accusations of witchcraft: committing crimes against men, forming an organized group, and having magical powers that could harm or heal a person. In fact, Kramer and Sprenger declared: "When a woman is alone, she thinks evil."

Salem: A Holocaust of Witches

The most notorious witch trials took place in 1692 in New England. What began as strange fits that many locals considered witchcraft ended as one of the most infamous events in US history:

the Salem witch trials. It is a gripping and fascinating story in its own right. The intensity of hysteria that spread throughout eastern Massachusetts that year held a power over life and death. More women were targeted than men. People were accused, hunted down, tortured, tried, charged, and killed. For many, their guilt or innocence will never be known.

The wall in front of this house depicts names of people killed during the Salem witch trials.

Bridget Bishop

Bridget Bishop once owned an apple orchard in Salem. Bishop did not fit the mold her society had made for her. Her scandalous behavior made her the subject of much talk of the town. At the time of the witch trials, she was in her third marriage. She had a bad reputation for entertaining visitors late at night and playing forbidden games, such as shuffleboard. It was this improper attitude that made her a prime target when witch accusations started to fly. Despite her insistence that, "I have no familiarity with the devil," Bishop was convicted of witchcraft. She was the first to die in the Salem witch trials, hanged on what would later become known as Gallows Hill.

Susannah Martin

At the time of the witch craze, Susannah Martin was a widowed mother of eight. Martin was no stranger to accusations of witchcraft by the time of the Salem witch trials. In the 1670s, she was accused of witchcraft and infanticide. (When her then husband sued her

accusers of slander, the charges were dropped.) However, in 1692, when fifteen of her neighbors accused her of bewitching them and killing their livestock, she had nobody to defend her.

Some historians theorize that Martin was accused at least in part because of her involvement in a disputed inheritance. Regardless of the reason, Martin was convicted. She apparently spent her last days reading "her worn old Bible" alone in her cell.

Dorothy Good

Like many Salem women in 1692, Dorothy Good was accused of witchcraft; unlike the other accused witches, Good was only four years old. After she was interrogated by the magistrates, Good admitted to being a witch and claimed that she had seen her mother speak with the devil. Good was also accused of being deranged by people who claimed to have been attacked by her. At age five, she was sent to prison, making her the youngest person to be imprisoned during the Salem witch trials.

Salem officials visited Good in jail, where she told them that she owned a snake that could talk to her and drank blood from her finger. The officials took this as evidence that the snake was her **familiar**, a witch's servant that usually takes an animal form. Good was held in prison for nearly nine months. On December 10, 1692, she was released, her case never brought to trial.

Forced End of an Era

As 1692 came to its close, the witch hysteria was losing its steam. The governor of the colony, William Phips, upon hearing that his own wife was accused of witchcraft, ordered an end to the trials, which had gotten out of hand. The last trial was held in January 1693, with

the death count of nineteen by hanging and one by being crushed by rocks. Phips also pardoned those found guilty and awaiting execution.

It was cold comfort when the Massachussetts General Court later overrode the guilty verdicts against the accused witches, holding them and their families blameless. Bitterness and suspicion lingered in a community torn apart by paranoia, fear, and revenge.

The Devil's Book

In April 1692, the girls Ann Putnam, Mercy Lewis, and Abigail Williams accused Giles Corey, a prosperous farmer and covenanted member of the church, of witchcraft. According to Ann Putnam's story, Giles Corey visited her one night in the form of a ghost and asked her to sign her name in "the devil's book." Puritan religion holds that a person made a pact with the devil by making their mark in the devil's book. A person only became a witch after signing their name. He or she then had demonic powers, including the ability to take on a ghostlike form and do harm to another. Evidence that the accused had signed the devil's book, either through confession or confirmation by an eyewitness, was an important element in witch trial proceedings.

This woodcut shows Giles Corey being accused of witchcraft by a witness at the Salem witch trials.

Several other young women came forward and described Corey as "a dreadful wizard" and recounted stories of assaults by his specter. Thus, as a matter of speculation, Corey was named a witch.

Corey was tortured with pressing to gain a confession. He was stripped and forced to lie down while a board was placed on his body and heavy stones gradually added to it. Corey maintained his innocence for two days as hundreds of pounds were piled on top of him. On the second day, the court asked if he would confess, to which Corey said, "More weight!" and died. He was buried in an unmarked grave.

FOLLOW THE YELLOW BRICK ROAD

"Now, the Wicked Witch of the West had but only one eye, yet that was as powerful as a telescope, and could see everywhere. So, as she sat in the door of her castle, she happened to look around and saw Dorothy lying asleep with her friends all about her. They were a long distance off, but the Wicked Witch was angry to find them in her country."

EXCERPT FROM L. FRANK BAUM'S 1900 VERSION OF
THE WONDERFUL WIZARD OF OZ

FAIRY TALES ARE A TYPE OF FOLKTALE or fable. In these enchanted stories are queens, giants, elves, princes, dragons, ogres, fairies, and witches—good and evil. The oldest fairy tales were told and retold for hundreds of years before they were written down. French fairy tales were the first to be collected and recorded, but now we can read fairy tales from almost any culture. What we do know of fairy tales is that people everywhere love stories in which truth rules over deception; generosity is rewarded; and love, mercy, and kindness prove to have great power.

Opposite: Margaret Hamilton as the Wicked Witch of the West (*left*) and Judy Garland as Dorothy Gale (*right*) in the iconic 1939 film *The Wizard of Oz.*

Green with Envy

The Wicked Witch of the West is a fictional character invented by L. Frank Baum, author of *The Wonderful Wizard of Oz*, published in 1900. She is introduced in the novel's twelfth chapter, "The Search for the Wicked Witch," in which Baum wrote her as the most significant antagonist, or hostile opponent, in the story. Baum never named his Wicked Witch; she is only known by her title of position. It wasn't until the classic 1939 Hollywood film *The Wizard of Oz* that the Wicked Witch became famous.

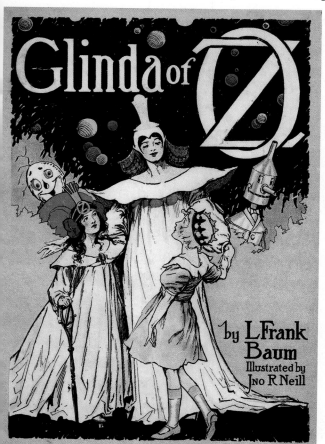

The cover of one of the original Oz stories by L. Frank Baum

Played by Margaret Hamilton, the character of the Wicked Witch was depicted with green "boogeyman" skin, a physical trait started in the film and continued in later literary and dramatic representations of witches. In Gregory McGuire's revisionist Oz novel, *Wicked: The Life and Times of the Wicked Witch of the West* (1995), the witch, Elphaba, is green because her mother consumed "Green Miracle Elixir" while she was pregnant with her. In the 2013 Disney film *Oz the Great and Powerful*, the pre–Wicked Witch of the West is a young and naive Good Witch named Theodora.

Her skin turns green from eating a green poison apple that causes her heart to shed all of its goodness. Theodora is thereby transformed into the same green-skinned villain from the 1939 film. In the popular television show

Once Upon a Time, Zelena is the Wicked Witch. Jealous over a newly arrived Dorothy, who became a threat to the prophecy involving Oz's four witches, she turned "green with envy."

In Baum's original book, the Wicked Witch's skin was not at all green. The book does, however, state: "The witch did not bleed where she was bitten, for she was so wicked that the blood in her had dried up many years before."

One Bad Witch

In folktales, witches usually take on the role of the villain. A supernatural male villain is usually identified as the devil or an ogre rather than a witch. The female character is often written as the wicked mother or stepmother who curses or enchants the tale's male and female protagonists, or the people in the story involved in conflict.

In the 1812 Brothers Grimm fairy tale "Hansel and Gretel," Hansel and Gretel are a young brother and sister threatened by a child-eating witch living deep in the forest. The witch lures the two inside her cottage, built of gingerbread and cakes and with windowpanes of clear sugar, with the promise of soft beds and delicious food. Tired and hungry, Hansel and Gretel are unaware that the witch's only plan is to come up with a way to cook and eat them. It soon becomes clear what her intention is, and the pair quickly try to combat her. Eventually, the witch gets too close to the fire in which she had planned to roast Hansel and Gretel. Gretel sees her opportunity:

> "We will bake first," said the [witch], "I have already heated the oven, and kneaded the dough." She pushed poor Gretel

out to the oven, from which flames of fire were already darting. "Creep in," said the witch, "and see if it is properly heated, so that we can put the bread in." And once Gretel was inside, she intended to shut the oven and let her bake in it, and then she would eat her, too.

But Gretel saw what she had in mind, and said, "I do not know how I am to do it. How do I get in?"

"Silly goose," said the old woman, "the door is big enough. Just look, I can get in myself." And she crept up and thrust her head into the oven.

Then Gretel gave [the witch] a push that drove her far into it, and shut the iron door, and fastened the bolt. Oh. Then she began to howl quite horribly, but Gretel ran away, and the godless witch was miserably burnt to death. Gretel, however, ran like lightning to Hansel, opened his little stable, and cried, "Hansel, we are saved. The old witch is dead."

This is an illustration from the classic fairy tale "Hansel and Gretel."

Once free, and knowing that they no longer have to fear the witch, Hansel and Gretel go "into the witch's house, and in every corner there stood chests full of pearls and jewels." On returning home, "Gretel empt[ies] her pinafore until pearls and precious stones r[u]n about the room, and Hansel thr[ows] one handful after another out of his pocket to add to them. Then all anxiety [is] at an end, and they live together in perfect happiness."

One Good Witch

The good witch has magical powers and functions to help the protagonist. She is often the daughter of a demon or another witch. Although she uses magic, she is not explicitly referred to as a witch. She is never an old hag with a hooked nose, and she does not fly using a broomstick.

Glinda, dubbed "The Good Witch of the South," is the most-loved "good" witch in folktales and classic film. Played by Billie Burke in movie adaptation *The Wizard of Oz*, Glinda is a beautiful young woman dressed in white with flowing red hair and bright blue eyes. Although she is much older than her beauty lets on, Glinda "knows how to keep young in spite of the many years she has lived."

According to Baum's book, Glinda lives in a palace near the southern border of the Quadling Country and has a large army of female soldiers (men are not prominent in her court.) She does not associate with any sort of evil or dark magic. She uses various tools, charms, and instruments from her workshop to practice her good magic and is quite protective of those who live in the South. Because she is never distracted by anything that might sully her goodness, Glinda serves as the moral compass in the Oz books.

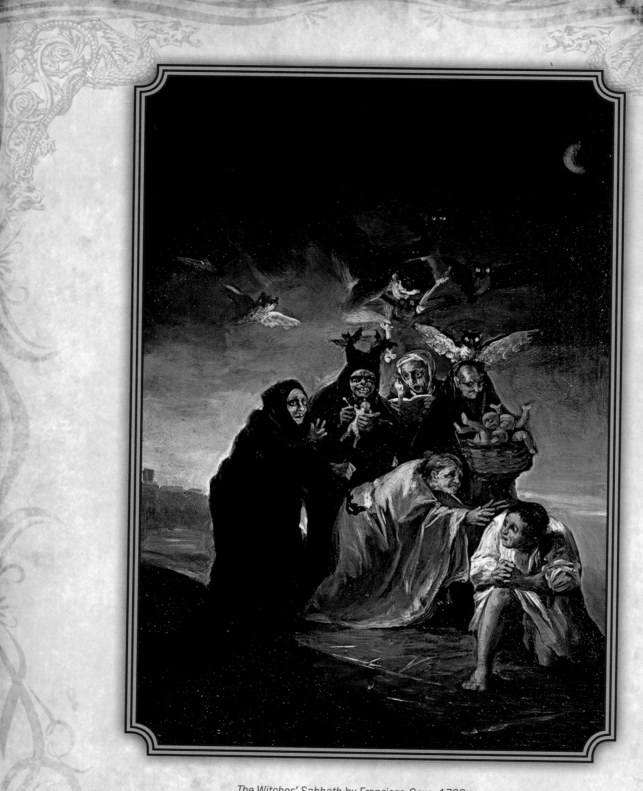

The Witches' Sabbath by Francisco Goya, 1798

Not an Ordinary Hag

Books, movies, comics, and cartoons have given us the idea of what to expect when we think of a witch: an old hag with a pointy hat and warts on her nose. However, this image would not be recognized by many people in different parts of the world. Strange-looking characters in outlandish costumes may be what they expect to see—but never a cackling hag.

Some people think of witches as looking completely ordinary, the only thing setting them apart being their secret knowledge of the magical arts. Yet there are several archetypes, or perfect examples, of witches: Male archetypes include the sorcerers and the warlocks in literature. Female archetypes include the feral child (one who resembles a wild beast) who lives in the wilderness, the love-spell practicing maiden, the gypsy or the fortune-teller, and the priestess of a goddess. However, the most classical is the hag. She is usually a crone-type, or old and ugly, and shuns society.

The crone-type is the most feared. She is viewed as a conjurer of evil spirits, a possessor of the evil eye, wise but cold, and ready to curse anyone who crosses her. Some are even said to eat babies. When full, the hag then uses the baby fat for making spell-casting candles. Ancient societies feared the malevolent witchcraft of hags because hags could be vampires as well as associated with demons or darkness. In some places there are special shamans, called witch doctors, who specifically work to counter the hags' magic and dark powers.

6

BLACK CATS AND MYTHS AND LEGENDS

"You see, a witch has to have a familiar—some little animal like a cat or a toad. He helps her somehow. When the witch dies the familiar is supposed to die too, but sometimes it doesn't. Sometimes, if it's absorbed enough magic, it lives on."

HENRY KUTTNER, *MASTERS OF HORROR*

WITCHES AND THE PRACTICE OF witchcraft are deeply rooted in history. Over the centuries, many interesting images and myths about witches and their lives have surfaced. Among the most common is the witch's familiar: the so-called evil black cat who serves as a partner in casting spells.

FELINE EVIL?

Cats were said to have supernatural powers that enabled them to sense spirits. Because they are difficult to see in dark places or at night, black cats made ideal familiars for witches, complimenting their masters' secretive activities well. Other times, black cats were

Opposite: Black cats have long been wrongly associated with witches and witchcraft. However, in many places, such as in Japan, black cats are considered good luck.

used as sacrifices in magic rituals. It was believed that witches themselves could transform into cats a total of nine times, giving rise to the superstition that cats have nine lives.

During the witch trials, ownership of a black cat was often interpreted as evidence of evil and witchcraft. People thought that a strange cat could sneak into a house and attack its sleeping inhabitants, sometimes killing them by smothering. In fact, because cats were found to be equally as guilty as their owners, they would be punished alongside them, typically by being burned alive. For modern Wiccans, cats are not sacrificed in their rituals. Wicca is a nature-oriented religion, and respect for animals is one of its most important principles. However, many witches today keep black cats as pets.

BLACK-CAT LORE

In other black-cat lore, if a cat jumps over a dead body, it is said the corpse will then become a vampire. Cats have also figured in medieval medicine. A cat boiled in oil could be used to dress wounds in the seventeenth century. The idea was that an illness would transfer to a house's cats, which could then be driven from the property, cleansing its occupants. Likewise, witches could use cats to cause plague. The recipe? One powdered cat, stuffed with fruits, herbs, and grain, tossed down over a town from a mountaintop.

Cats could also be beneficial fertility charms. Burying a cat in a field was said to ensure a bountiful harvest. However, just as a cat could be used to heal as well as cause plague, a witch could use a cat stuffed with vegetables and placed in a river to destroy crops. After three days, the witch would retrieve the cat, dry it, ground it, and scatter the powder over the fields.

A "Familiar" Tale

Like many pet owners, witches cherished the cats that accompanied them. Anyone who harmed a witch's companion placed themselves in harm's way, as told in this sixteenth-century tale recorded on the online witch site Oocities.org:

> In the Lake District in England, there lived a witch whose cat was killed by the innkeeper's dog. The old woman stood by, sad but dry-eyed (witches could not weep), while the innkeeper's servant dug a grave for the animal. The old woman asked the servant, whose name was Willan, to read some verses over the cat from a book she had, a request that sent the man into howls of laughter. He threw the small, furry body into the hole he had dug, reciting in a loud voice a silly, mocking rhyme: "Ashes to ashes and dust to dust. Here's a hole and go thou must."
>
> "Very well," said the old woman bitterly. "You will be punished, as you will see."
>
> And Willan was indeed punished. A day later, as he was plowing the innkeeper's field, the plowshare caught in a rock on the ground; the handles flew up into the air and pierced the young man's eyes. He was blinded for life.

"I'm Melting! Melting!"

Another common myth is that a witch can be destroyed by water. Thanks much in part to Baum and *The Wizard of Oz*, water has been the symbol for a witch's tortuous demise.

In the film *The Wizard of Oz*, the wizard, Oz, tells Dorothy that he cannot help her and her friends—Lion, Scarecrow, and

Tin-Man—unless she kills the Wicked Witch of the West. Later in the movie, after being held captive by the Wicked Witch, Dorothy manages to toss a bucket of water on her—albeit by mistake. As she melts away to nothing, the Wicked Witch of the West curses:

> You cursed brat! Look what you've done! I'm melting! Melting! Oh, what a world! What a world! Who would have thought a good little girl like you could destroy my beautiful wickedness? Oooooh, look out! I'm going! Oooooh! Oooooooh!

The water burns the witch's skin like acid, for reasons that have never been explained. Some have said that because the witch was so evil, a substance such as water was simply too pure for her old, bloodless body. It can also be said that water destroyed the Wicked Witch because she is a "fire" witch. In the 1939 film, the Wicked Witch is capable of creating hot energy in her hand that forms fire balls and smoke from her broomstick. Thus water—the opposing force of fire—would be her enemy.

On the other hand, Glinda, the good witch, is a water witch. In fact, she was able to create snowfall with her magic wand and a strong mist in Oz. Since Glinda is a good, water-based witch and the Wicked Witch is a bad, fire-based witch, the two are polar opposites. Where the Wicked Witch met her watery demise, Glinda the Good Witch could not be destroyed.

Trial by Water

An ancient practice that confirmed a so-called witch's guilt was a "trial by water." A suspected witch would be dragged to a body of

George Wharton Edwards

water, stripped, and her hands tied. The spectators would then toss her in to determine her fate. It was thought that in accepting the devil's magic, witches had foregone their Christian baptism. The water a witch was placed in would reject her body, and she would float harmlessly on the surface. Only the innocent sank. However, both outcomes proved tragic. Those who floated were immediately executed. Those who sank often accidentally drowned.

Many women suffered punishments in the 1600s. Many witches were placed in a dunking chair like this one and given a trial by water.

This illustration shows Matthew Hopkins, a witchfinder. Between 1644 and 1646, Hopkins and a pair of assistants traveled through the counties of Norfolk, Essex, and Suffolk, performing brutal tortures in their search for suspected sorcerers.

Dessert, Anyone?

In a bizarre eighteenth-century effort to counter a witch's evil magic, the "witch cake" was concocted to identify so-called evildoers. If a person claimed that his or her mysterious illness was brought on by a witch's curse or if a person had become possessed, witch-hunters would then take a sample of their urine. This sample would then be taken to a baker, usually a slave, who mixed it with rye-meal and baked it into a cake. One of the witch's familiars was then force-fed the horrible dessert. Under the effects of the dessert's spell, the familiar would be forced to reveal the guilty witch's identity.

Witch cakes came into play during the Salem witch trials, when the slave Tituba baked one to root out the person responsible for terrorizing the possessed girls. At age nine, Betty, daughter of Salem Village minister Samuel Parris, was curious about who she would marry and if he would be wealthy. She and her cousin Abigail then experimented with fortune telling using a superstitious object called a Venus glass. The glass allowed the girls to observe an egg white floating in a glass of water. The Venus glass would manipulate the shape of the egg, forming a symbol that would foretell the observer's future. This curiosity led to them being accused of witchcraft.

Tituba's plan was only half-baked, however, and the cake backfired. Not only were the girls found not guilty, but Tituba's use of the witch cake served as evidence against her when she herself was later accused of practicing witchcraft.

7

MODERN-DAY AND MEMORABLE WITCHES

"We're everywhere, out there, among you."

C. J. MORROW, *THE FINDER*

MORE THAN THREE HUNDRED YEARS have passed since the infamous Salem witch trials, and much of what was known about, or thought of, witches and witchcraft has changed. Witchcraft is a **pagan religion**. Pagan religions include those that are not Christianity, Judaism, or Islam, such as Hinduism, Buddhism, Taoism, Confucianism, and more. Many pagan religions are nature-oriented, such as the many Native American religions. Because Wicca worships Earth and nature, it is considered to be a pagan religion. It was created in the 1940s and 1950s by Gerald Brosseau Gardner (1884–1964), who defined witchcraft as "a positive and life-affirming religion that includes divination, herblore, magic and psychic abilities." Wiccans, or practitioners of Wicca, take an oath to do no harm with their craft. As of 2008, the Wiccan population was

Opposite: Maleficent, played by Angelina Jolie (2014)

over 342,000, according to an ABC News article, but that number has likely since increased. There are many shops and stores that cater to the Wiccan faith, too, making it a more accessible and accepted practice than witchcraft was in centuries past.

The Magic of Hollywood

Fictional witches have a long history in both movies and television, and they span the spectrum from good to evil. The best witch characters stick with us long after we have watched them, and we continue to ponder their magical powers. Here's a look at a few.

Cassie Nightingale, *The Good Witch*

"I will not dream of Jake Russell. I will not dream of Jake Russell." A truly good witch with great intentions, her real name is Sue-Ellen Brock. She was born to performers who traveled all over Europe. Cassie describes it as a "magical time" in her life. Her parents died in a car crash outside Zürich, and she was sent to a foster family in the United States. Her foster family was so strict they "killed the magic," so she ran away—that is, until she found Grey House.

Maleficent, *Sleeping Beauty*

"You poor, simple fools. Thinking you could defeat me. Me! The mistress of all evil!" Dubbed the Mistress of All Evil, Maleficent is the antagonist of Walt Disney's 1959 film *Sleeping Beauty*. Maleficent curses the king and queen's baby, Aurora, after they do not invite the witch to their daughter's christening. Her curse dooms Aurora to die before her sixteenth birthday. Not only is her look foreboding, but also her motives in the film are unmatched when it comes to witchcraft. Maleficent is undoubtedly one of the most sinister Disney villains to date and a witch that no one would want to anger.

Endora, *Bewitched*

"I know what a bat is. Those ugly flying things people think we're always cooking." More mischievous and meddling than evil, Endora terrorized the Stephens household in the classic TV show *Bewitched* (1964–1972). A magical twist on the disapproving mother-in-law, Endora focused her powers on the unsuspecting mortal Darrin, a New York City advertising executive who married her daughter, Samantha.

Willow Rosenberg, *Buffy the Vampire Slayer*

"This is creepy. I don't like the thought that there's a vampire out there that looks like me." As one of the main characters on *Buffy the Vampire Slayer* (1997–2003), Willow Rosenberg found her place in the gang by teaching herself how to practice magic. She was introduced to the forces of magic by attempting a complex spell to "re-ensoul" Angel. During the ritual, Willow tapped into considerable power that would lead her to the practice of witchcraft.

Melisandre, *Game of Thrones*

"I see a darkness in you. And in that darkness, eyes staring back at me. Brown eyes, blue eyes, green eyes. Eyes you'll shut forever. We will meet again." Born a slave in Essos and often referred to as The Red Woman, Melisandre shook up the TV series *Game of Thrones* (2011–) as an eastern priestess with an attitude. Claiming potent abilities like the power of prophecy, Melisandre successfully converted other characters to her religion and gained political power in the process. As a Red Priestess of the Lord of the Light, Melisandre is not a witch to cross.

Minerva McGonagall, Harry Potter Series

"Hogwarts is threatened! Man the boundaries. Protect us! Do your duty to our school!" Professor McGonagall is first depicted as reserved and proper, but throughout the Harry Potter series she becomes unveiled as a fierce and powerful witch. A member of the First and Second Order of the Phoenix, she puts her life on the line time and time again to defend Hogwarts from evil. Following the war against the evil wizard Voldemort, McGonagall took over as Headmistress of Hogwarts, where she worked for a decade.

Winnie Sanderson, *Hocus Pocus*

"You know, I've always wanted a child. And now I think I'll have one … on toast!" Winifred "Winnie" Sanderson is the primary antagonist in the Disney Halloween-themed film *Hocus Pocus* (1993). The oldest of the three Sanderson Sisters—all villains— Winifred, described as bossy, is the most prominent.

The Sanderson Sisters were three women who were convicted of witchcraft during the Salem witch trials and hanged on All Hollow's Eve (October 31), 1693. Three hundred years later, on the anniversary of their deaths (Halloween), Max, a skeptical teenager who thinks that their legend is just a load of hogwash, resurrects the witches. Reborn in the mid-1990s, the sisters strike out to wreak havoc.

Winifred displays a variety of powers, including the ability to conjure lightning from her palms. She, like most fictional witches, has the ability to fly using a broom. Winifred also possesses unusual strength for a witch, capable of lifting Max and his friends with minimal effort and tossing them. Lastly, Winifred has a repertoire of spells that allow her to do nearly everything, from bewitching people to reanimating rotten corpses.

URSULA, *The Little Mermaid*

"I admit that in the past I've been a nasty. They weren't kidding when they called me, well, a witch." The wicked sea witch Ursula in Disney's *The Little Mermaid* (1989) is undoubtedly powerful. Along with the ability to grow into an enormous beast and steal voices, Ursula also possesses what may be the greatest evil cackle of any witch, which helped to set her up as a fan favorite among the many classic Disney villains. Ursula also uses her talent as a smooth talker to manipulate the unsuspecting Merfolk. Her potions are also extremely powerful, able to physically transform people, including the heroine Ariel when she wishes she could be human. Ursula also changes herself, such as when she transforms into Vanessa (Ariel's evil twin), and even into a massive sea monster.

SABRINA SPELLMAN, *Sabrina the Teenage Witch*

"There's no motivation like desperation!" Although Sabrina Spellman from *Sabrina the Teenage Witch* (1996–2003) was not an evil, cruel, or scary witch, there is no denying her power. Sabrina could turn people into animals, travel to other dimensions, fly on a vacuum cleaner (the modernized broomstick), and do just about anything she wanted. What made Sabrina a witch to remember? Learning to be a great witch while also struggling with being a teenager.

Witches Among Us

The history of witches is a fascinating subject. They have suffered bad reputations, been misunderstood and tortured, and sentenced to death. They are judged by myths, preconceptions, and fear. Yet practitioners of witchcraft remain among us. Although several mysteries regarding witches are yet to be solved and some cannot decide whether their existence is real, witches are here—in the magic called "life."

GLOSSARY

adherent A person who gives support or loyalty to a leader, belief, or group.

credulous Too ready to believe things; easily fooled or cheated.

divination The practice of reading signs and symbols in special objects, such as tarot cards, bones, or tea leaves, that foretell the future.

excommunication Exclusion from fellowship in a group or community; usually a church.

familiar The spiritual servant of a witch, usually in animal form.

heretical Of, relating to, or characterized by departure from accepted beliefs or standards.

incantation A series of words said as a magic spell or charm.

incubus An evil spirit that lies on persons in their sleep.

Inquisition A historical organization within the Catholic Church that rooted out and punished people who went against the church's beliefs.

malady A disease or ailment.

malevolent Having or showing a wish to do evil to others; malicious.

Middle Ages The period of European history from about 500 CE to about 1500 CE.

mystical Inspiring a sense of spiritual mystery, awe, and fascination; resulting from prayer or deep thought.

pagan religion Religions other than the main world religions of Christianity, Judaism, or Islam.

peasantry The social class constituted by peasants, meaning the class constituted by small farmers and tenants, sharecroppers, and laborers.

poltergeist A ghost that makes strange noises and causes objects to move.

sect A division or group; regarding witchcraft, a specific group of witches.

secular Of, relating to, or controlled by the government rather than by the church.

sorcery The use of magic, especially black magic.

temporal Of or relating to earthly life.

treatise A book or article that discusses a subject carefully and thoroughly.

voodoo A religion that arose during the slave trade that combines Roman Catholicism with traditional West African beliefs and rituals; many elements of voodoo involve magic and sorcery.

Wicca A religion that is characterized by belief in the existence of magical powers in nature.

To Learn More about Witches

Books

Doeden, Matt. *The Salem Witch Trials: An Interactive History Adventure*. You Choose: History. North Mankato, MN: Capstone Press, 2011.

Graves, Lisa. *History's Witches*. Irvine, CA: Xist Publishing, 2013.

Martin, Michael J., and Brian Bascle. *The Salem Witch Trials*. Graphic History. North Mankato, MN: Capstone Press, 2005.

Website

Salem Witch Trials

kids.nationalgeographic.com/kids/stories/history/salem-witch-trials

Discover more about the witch craze that swept the small Puritan community of Salem Village, Massachusetts, in 1692.

Video

History of Halloween Videos

www.history.com/topics/halloween/history-of-halloween/videos/history-of-witches

Watch this series of videos and learn how witches were perceived as evil beings by early Christians in Europe, inspiring the iconic Halloween figure.

Bibliography

Baum, L. Frank. *The Wonderful Wizard of Oz*. New York: Geo M. Hill Co., 1900.

Cabot, Laurie. *Power of the Witch*. New York: Random House, 1990.

Carlson, Laurie Winn. *A Fever in Salem: A New Interpretation of the New England Witch Trials*. Chicago: Ivan R. Dee, 1999.

Day, Christian. *The Witches' Book of the Dead*. San Francisco: Weiser Books, 2011.

Ehrenreich, Barbara, and Deirdre English. *Witches, Midwives, and Nurses: A History of Women Healers*. New York: The Feminist Press at CUNY, 2010.

Godbeer, Richard. *Escaping Salem: The Other Witch Hunt of 1692*. New Narratives in American History. New York: Oxford University Press, 2005.

Günzel, Anne Sophie. *Witchcraft in Early Modern Germany*. Norderstedt, Germany: GRIN Verlag GmbH, 2004.

Haase, Donald, ed. *The Greenwood Encyclopedia of Folktales and Fairy Tales*. Westport, CT: Greenwood Press, 2008.

Hill, Douglass. *Witches & Magic-Makers*. New York: DK Eyewitness Books, 2000.

Ingram, Martin Van Buren. *An Authenticated History of the Famous Bell Witch*. Rockville, MD: Wildside Press, 2009.

Karlsen, Carol F. *The Devil in the Shape of a Woman: Witchcraft in Colonial New England*. New York: Norton Paperback, 1998.

Nardo, Don. *The Salem Witch Trials*. American History. Farmington Hills, MI: Gale, Cengage Learning, 2007.

Purkiss, Diane. *The Witch in History: Early Modern and Twentieth-Century Representations*. New York: Routledge, 1996.

Roach, Marilynne K. *Six Women of Salem: The Untold Story of The Accused and Their Accusers in the Salem Witch Trials*. Philadelphia: Da Capo Press, 2013.

Rowe, Catherine, ed. *The Penguin Book of Witches*. New York: Penguin Group, 2014.

Russell, Jeffrey B., and Alexander Brooks. *A History of Witchcraft: Sorcerers, Heretics & Pagans*. New York: Thames & Hudson, Inc., 2007.

Index

About the Author

Cynthia A. Roby is the author of several fictional short stories as well as nonfiction books for young readers. She has held a curiosity for witches since her first view of the classic film *The Wizard of Oz*. Roby currently lives in New York City with her two familiars, Peter Tosh and Toni Morrison.